Preface

Do astronauts from outer space visit the Earth in "flying saucers" or "UFOs"? Did they visit us in the past and did our ancestors think they were some sort of gods because of their advanced technology? Did people 2000 years ago use electric batteries? Why can the continent of Antarctica be found on some medieval maps even though history books tell us it was only discovered two centuries ago? Can some people predict catastrophes or see into the future — perhaps with the help of astrology? Do the ghosts of murder victims really haunt old castles? Do gigantic creatures like giant squids inhabit the depths of the oceans — unknown to and undiscovered by scientists?

This **start me up!**™ book examines these questions and any information we have regarding them. They all have one thing in common:

there is no clear or definitive answer to any of them. Many people believe in UFOs, astrology, prophecy, ghosts, and in many other events in the skies, in the human brain, or even in the "realm of the dead," but these are all matters that require more investigation.

Scientists, of course, are skeptical. There have been many claims of mysterious phenomena, but even after decades of research there is still no convincing proof that these beliefs are justified. Unfortunately this is an area in which there are many swindlers and cheats waiting to deceive unsuspecting victims.

This book makes no attempt to offer definitive answers to any of these questions. It does try, however, to offer a serious treatment of the wide and colorful world of believable and unbelievable phenomena.

Volume 4

PUBLISHERS: Tessloff Publishing, Quadrillion Media LLC

EDITOR: Alan Swensen

PICTURE SOURCES:

PHOTOS: Action press/Merchandising, Hamburg: p. 9, Photoreporters p. 9; Archiv für Kunst und Geschichte, Berlin: pp. 19, 20, 22, 32; Museum of Baghdad, Iraq: p. 18; Bavaria Bildagentur, Gauting: pp. 4, 46; Bibliothèque Nationale de Paris: p. 23; Bildarchiv Preussischer Kulturbesitz, Berlin: pp. 13, 16, 22, 26, 27, 29, 31, 42, 48; Bildagentur Schuster, Oberursel: pp. 8, 17, 30, 33, 35, 38, 39; Deutscher Wetterdienst, Offenbach: p. 7; dpa, Frankfurt: pp. 5, 6, 37; Elsler Historisches Farbarchiv, Norderney: pp. 29, 36; Helga Lade Fotoagentur / N. Fischer: p. 43; Mary Evans Picture Library, London: p. 40; pandis media gmbh/Daily Mail, London: p. 46; Pre-Columbian Art Research Institute / Dr. Merle Green Robertson: p. 12; South American Pictures, Woodbridge Suffolk: pp. 10, 11; Ullstein Bilderdienst, Berlin: p. 21; ZEFA Bildagentur, Dusseldorf: p. 28

ILLUSTRATIONS: Frank Kliemt: pp. 13, 17, 19, 23; Peter Klaucke: pp. 1, 3, 4/5, 14/15, 24/25, 28, 30/31, 34, 36/37, 44

Translated by Lori Childs-Koerner

Copyright: © MCMXCVIII Tessloff Publishing, Burgschmietstrasse 2-4, 90419 Nuremberg, Germany

© MCMXCVIII Quadrillion Media LLC, 10105 East Via Linda Road, Suite 103-390, Scottsdale AZ 85258, USA

Visit us on the World Wide Web at http://www.quadrillionusa.com

Library of Congress Cataloging-in-Publication Data is available.

ISBN 1-58185-003-4

Printed in Belgium

Printing 10 9 8 7 6 5 4 3 2 1

Table of Contents

Contact With Extraterrestrials

What are UFOs? 4

When was the first UFO sighted? 5

How reliable are reports of UFO sightings? 6

What do extraterrestrials look like? 8

Have space travelers visited the Earth before? 10

Are Daniken's claims plausible? 12

Mysteries of the Past

Did Atlantis actually exist? 13

Is Stonehenge a prehistoric observatory? 16

Was the "machine of Antikythera" an ancient computer? 17

Were electric batteries already in use 2,000 years ago? 18

What did ancient civilizations know about the Earth? 19

Did people from the "Old World" visit the Americas in ancient times? 21

What surprises are hidden in old maps? 22

Looking Into the Future

Where did astrology originate? 24

What does a horoscope look like? 26

Do the stars tell the truth? 27

What other methods of telling the future are there? 28

How did the Oracle at Delphi work? 31

Who was Nostradamus? 32

Forces From the Hereafter

Where can you find ghosts? 33

What are ghosts? 35

How do mediums try to contact the dead? 37

How seriously can we take séances? 39

What is psi? 40

Can the existence of extrasensory abilities be proven? 41

Can dowsers find water and gold? 42

Mysterious Animals

Do unknown monsters live in the depths of the oceans? 45

What is the Loch Ness Monster? 46

Is there really a Yeti in the Himalayan Mountains? 46

Have we discovered all of the animals on Earth? 47

Index 48

This is what aliens look like in science fiction films. They are, of course, no more than products of moviemakers' imaginations.

Contact With Extraterrestrials

What are UFOs?

It is shortly before midnight on October 18, 1973. Helicopter pilot Larry Coyne and his small crew are on a routine flight near Mansfield, Ohio. Suddenly the helicopter is enveloped by red light. While the surprised Coyne searches for the source, a red glowing object appears next to his helicopter. He tries in vain to evade it. It hovers next to the craft, motionless. Then without warning a green light illuminates the cabin and the mysterious object disappears without a sound. At the same time the radio goes dead and the helicopter is drawn up several feet by some unseen force. Finally the pilot manages to regain control.

This report is just one example of the many unsolved encounters with UFOs, "Unidentified Flying Objects." For fifty years people have been reporting such sight-ings — among them experienced observers such as pilots and ship captains. They usually see bright balls or disks that suddenly appear in the sky, pause momentarily, and then speed across the heavens with incredible speed, disappearing as quickly as they appeared.

Hundreds of photographs of such mysterious objects have been offered to newspapers and magazines and some have even been published.

An explanation for these mysterious observations soon sprang up: they were spaceships used by inhabitants of far away solar systems to visit us — from planets technologically superior to ours. That would explain not only their incredible flying skills but also their ability to appear out of nowhere and disappear just as mysteriously. These extraterrestrial beings only wanted to observe and study us. They were not yet ready to make direct contact.

Laser beams used by discos often create effects in the night sky that could be mistaken for UFOs.

MANY SCIENTISTS BELIEVE that Earth is not the only planet where life has developed and that intelligent beings probably exist elsewhere in space as well. After all, there are 100 billion suns in our Milky Way alone and certainly millions of planets similar to Earth. For this reason radio telescopes continuously survey space for signs of intelligent extraterrestrial life — so far without success.

The crew of a UFO kidnapping people with their space ship. Have such strange encounters with aliens already taken place?

UFO SIGHTINGS have been reported all over the world, but especially in the United States and Europe. The idea that such objects might be spaceships from alien planets is a recent one. As long as there have been human beings, however, they have certainly seen things in the sky they couldn't understand — strange natural phenomena such as polar lights, sheet lightning, and meteorites. In earlier times they probably interpreted these phenomena as the work of gods or demons.

When was the first UFO sighted?

We can document the beginning of the UFO phenomenon precisely. On July 24, 1947 an American pilot named Kenneth Arnold saw nine unusual flying objects over the California mountains. "They flew like saucers skipping over the water," he later explained. Newspaper reporters quickly picked up Arnold's description and the expression "flying saucers" was born. Many people read the article and reported also having seen disk-shaped flying objects. All at once the flying objects were appearing all around the world at all times of the day and especially at night.

Soon a few people even claimed that strange humanoid beings got out of the UFOs and spoke to them, offering to fly them through outer space. One person stood out in particular: George Adamski who claimed to be from the famous Mount Palomar Observatory in California. He published several books about his trips in UFOs and millions of copies were sold worldwide.

Others reported they had been kidnapped and taken aboard UFOs and that strange operations were performed on them. Of course no one could show any traces of these treatments, even though large rewards were offered for such proof.

A student took this picture in New Mexico in 1967. The UFO allegedly made no sound and disappeared in a flash.

5

This photograph of a UFO was also taken in New Mexico. Unfortunately there are not many details visible on the strange object in the middle of the picture.

Surveys show that more than one fifth of all people firmly believe in the existence of spaceships from other planets. Many even report seeing UFOs themselves. The heads of observatories and planetariums receive phone calls almost daily from people who claim to have seen UFOs.

How reliable are reports of UFO sightings?

Many photographs of UFOs subsequently turn out to be fakes. It is very easy, for example, to throw a toy model of a UFO into the air and illuminate it, or to paste a picture of a UFO onto a windowpane and photograph it. However, such photographs are only published if the deception is not noticed immediately. Perhaps this is why almost all UFO photographs are out of focus!

Scientists who study the stars — astronomers — are rather doubtful, and they have good reason to be. After all, they are the ones who observe the sky almost every night —

one of them should have seen a UFO through a telescope or a camera a long time ago. But they have never seen one.

The United States Air Force came to the same conclusion. The military began paying very close attention right after the first UFO sightings. After all, it is one of their duties to monitor air space. At that time there was a great deal of political tension between the United States and Russia, and one of these "unidentified flying objects" could have been the result of some new Soviet missile or airplane technology.

Of course it turned out that there were very simple explanations for the majority of these UFO sightings. They were often optical illusions. What people had seen were bright stars or planets, high-flying airplanes or weather balloons, rock-

THE ROSWELL FIND

In the summer of 1947 a UFO supposedly crashed and was recovered together with its dead crew by U. S. armed forces near Roswell, New Mexico — also the location of a secret weapons test site. Some who believe in UFOs claim that the government tried to suppress reports of the event and keep the whole affair secret. In reality, a test balloon being developed by the Air Force for espionage purposes had crashed. Since the project was top secret, the government tried to keep the accident as quiet as possible.

This UFO, probably nothing more than an oval-shaped cloud, appeared over a farmhouse in South Korea in 1995.

In 1995 a film turned up that claimed to show a medical examination of one of the extraterrestrials that had crashed near Roswell in 1947. A curiously child-like, hairless figure with six fingers and a distended belly can be seen on the black-and-white strip of film. An examination of details of the film soon showed that it was a crude fake and not evidence of an extraterrestrial!

Clouds often take on oval forms and then look like "flying saucers" when you see them from the side.

et parts reentering Earth's atmosphere or shooting stars. There is even a cloud form (lenticular clouds) that strongly resembles a "flying saucer." Many UFOs seen at night turned out to be the lights of passing cars reflecting off wet streetcar cables or headlights hitting low clouds. Today the laser beams some discos use at night are sometimes mistaken for UFOs.

Even experts are sometimes mistaken. This is true of the UFO that helicopter pilot Larry Coyne saw. Extensive investigations and interviews with his crew revealed what had really happened. They lost radio contact because the helicopter was flying too low and the surrounding mountains blocked the radio waves. The "UFO" was actually a meteorite crashing to Earth, a chunk of rock from outer space that burned as it passed through the Earth's atmosphere — turning it into a red-hot ball of fire. The meteorite did not cause the sudden upward movement, however, but rather Coyne himself: the meteor startled him, and so he pulled the control stick towards himself in order to climb and not crash to Earth. This was an instinctive reaction but one that he could not remember afterwards. Of course, the meteorite was not suspended in the air, either. When he moved the control stick it caused the helicopter to turn such that the ball of fire appeared to stand still. All this happened in a fraction of a second but for the crew it seemed much longer. And the green light? That came from the green sunscreen at the top of the helicopter window. In rotating, the helicopter turned its upper part towards the meteorite for a moment and its light entered the cockpit through the green shade.

Of course there have always been and always will be people simply trying to get attention with their UFO stories. Upon closer examination it turned out that the alleged "UFO traveler" Adamski didn't belong to the Mount Palomar Observatory at all — he ran a snack shop on the road leading to the observatory and he had made up all the stories. That didn't hurt his book sales, however, and many people since then have been very successful with invented UFO stories.

All of the UFO photographs publicized so far have also turned out to be forgeries. For years American UFO researchers have offered large rewards for irrefutable proof of the existence of a spaceship — so far without success. Nevertheless, all of these investigations and exposed frauds have not stopped millions of people from continuing to believe in visitors from outer space. Evidently many people today find it comforting to believe that we are not alone in the universe.

What do extraterrestrials look like?

It isn't at all certain that there are other living beings in the universe besides us. Many scientists believe that the genesis of life on Earth resulted from a chain of events so random that it is very unlikely it could have happened twice. But if we consider the fact that there are a hundred billion suns in the Milky Way alone, then it is not too far fetched to believe that life could have evolved on a few other planets.

If there are other beings, however, there is no reason we should think they look like us. There have been too many accidental occurrences in the course of human evolution for this to be likely. The probability that this process oc-curred in exactly the same way somewhere else is virtually zero. For this reason alone we should be very skeptical of reports by UFO believers of encounters with humanoid beings.

If we want to picture what visitors from outer space might look like, it will take a considerable stretch of the imagination. It is unlikely that they would resemble any of the millions of life forms on Earth. On the other hand they are subject to the same laws of nature that we are, since these are true for the entire universe. Consequently they would need the help of high-ly developed technology in order to get here. In other words, they would have to cope with the immense distances between the stars, with planetary gravity, and with the vacuum of space. To do this

COMMUNICATING WITH EXTRATERRESTRIALS would certainly be very difficult. It is very unlikely that alien visitors would even recognize our speech as a method of communication — unless they have ears like ours. They probably wouldn't be able to produce sounds like our speech either. We cannot understand or speak with dolphins or apes, much less ants or snails — and these are our close relatives compared to extraterrestrials!

Radio telescopes like these in New Mexico can pick up even extremely weak cosmic signals. So far they have not received any signals from intelligent life elsewhere in the universe.

SCIENCE FICTION FILM-MAKERS in Hollywood and elsewhere have made many attempts over the years to portray extraterrestrial beings that do not look like Earth creatures. Usually they borrow ideas from the animal world (Alf, ET, Alien, and Independence Day). This is even true of the imaginative creatures that appear in the "Star Wars" films. The television series "Star Trek" did attempt to portray silicon-based life forms — according to scientists, this is the most likely alternative to Earth's carbon-based life forms — but such attempts were rare. It is clearly very difficult for us to imagine truly alien organisms. If such beings did come to Earth we might not even recognize them as life forms. Who knows — maybe there are extraterrestrials already among us and we are not aware of them.

they would need spaceships with the appropriate propulsion systems. They could not develop these, however, without a great deal of intelligence or without some kind of "manipulating organs" (like our hands and fingers). A beak and claws wouldn't be enough.

They would be able to move about to find and process raw materials. They would be able to "see" what they are doing — whether within the realm of light visible to us or at other wavelengths. They would probably be able to perceive depth, and this means they would need at least two eyes.

They would be able to "talk" to each other since it would be impossible for a single being to complete this task alone. It would not have to be a language as we understand it, however — that is, it wouldn't have to use sounds. They might communicate by means of light signals as lightening bugs do, by means of electrical

ET, the alien with a turtle-like face, is the hero of a popular movie.

impulses as some fish do, or by means of chemical signals as ants do.

Astronomers believe visits from outer space are highly unlikely. They are familiar with the tremendous distances of space — even traveling at the speed of light it would take four years to reach the nearest sun! A spaceship entering our solar system would have to be very lucky to find us at all. They would not be able to tell whether our solar system had an inhabited planet until they were very close.

And they would have had to land at exactly the right time. The Earth has existed for 4,600 million years and most of the time it was only full of microscopic little animals. Humans have only been around for about one hundred thousand years. If we were to imagine the entire existence of Earth as a single year, then humans did not exist until a few seconds before midnight on December 31st! It has only been the last few decades that space travelers would have found anyone on Earth who could comprehend space travel and extraterrestrial beings.

Could aliens possibly look like this? The shaggy alien Alf is stranded on Earth and has made friends here.

Perhaps space travelers visited the Earth thousands of years ago and spoke to our ancestors. They, of course, knew nothing of outer space and they certainly could not comprehend advanced technology. That is why they probably thought that these powerful visitors were gods. At least that is what the Swiss author Erich von Daniken has claimed now for years. His first book, "Chariots of the Gods?," which was published in 1968, made him famous overnight. In this book he claims that many things archaeologists find puzzling are in reality only clumsy depictions or accounts of events our ancestors couldn't comprehend.

Have space travelers visited the Earth before?

Although Daniken was not the first person to make such claims and almost all of the arguments in his book came from other authors, his book nevertheless caused quite a stir around the world. The time was probably right for such a theory: the United States was racing to put a man on the Moon. In many peoples' minds the door to the universe was opening. Besides, the book was exciting to read and fired peoples' imaginations. Daniken went on to write many other books that present similar ideas.

Daniken offered a lot of proof for his theory. If we can believe him, extraterrestrials have not only visited the Earth but have also had

Archaeologists are still puzzled by these gigantic pictures scratched into the ground in Nazca, Peru.

enormous influence on earthly events. These "gods" from other worlds changed our genetic make-up with gene technology that made us more intelligent. They helped build the Egyptian pyramids, taught us astronomy, agriculture, and medicine, and they took certain chosen humans with them on short trips into space. He even traced events in the Bible back to extraterrestrials: they punished humans with a great flood (and warned Noah by radio-telephone!). They visited the

This depiction of a human being, carved in stone, comes from South America. Daniken claims such pictures show prehistoric space travelers.

AN AMERICAN AUTHOR, CHARLES FORT, may have been the first writer to suggest that aliens visited our planet in ancient times. He lived from 1874 to 1932 and spent many years going through libraries looking for reports of strange phenomena. His imaginative books have stimulated many authors since then.

At first glance, these long lines scratched into the ground in the Nazca desert look like runways from some prehistoric airport.

A THEORY that often accompanies claims about visitors from space in ancient times is one that asserts that our advanced technological civilization was not the first one on Earth. According to this theory even more highly developed cultures existed before ours. These civilizations supposedly destroyed themselves or were exterminated by natural catastrophes. Only obscure signs and fragments of their secret, dangerously powerful knowledge survived the dark, less civilized times since then.

prophet Ezekiel in a spaceship. Using a "manna machine" they fed Moses and the Israelites during the 40 years of their wanderings in the desert. They destroyed Sodom and Gomorrah with a kind of atomic bomb.

At first glance, the large number of Daniken's claims is overwhelming. You can find cave paintings of humanoid beings wearing something like a space helmet with antennas on top. Were these drawings of extraterrestrials who had to protect themselves from Earth's atmosphere or bacteria?

In many places on Earth we are awed by massive walls and enormous structures made of stones weighing tons. They were built in a time before the crane was invented.

About 3,200 years ago the Egyptians in the city of Thebes erected a statue of Ramses that weighs about 1,000 tons. The inhabitants of the Easter Islands

set up dozens of mysterious looking stone figures, each weighing several tons. In Nazca in Peru there are curious straight lines cut into the ground that go on for a mile or more and look like the remains of ancient runways. In Palenque, Mexico archaeologists found a drawing on stone that depicts a Mayan priest. At first glance it looks like he is sitting on some kind of rocket.

Besides these examples, old texts — including the Bible — mention strange celestial phenomena. Daniken sees these as reports by people who had experienced things and seen objects they could not begin to comprehend, things they could not explain and for which they had no words. They attempted to explain what they had experienced with the words available to them. Not until today, in this age of space travel, could we begin to understand the meaning of these reports.

Stone statues weighing several tons look out over the ocean from the Easter Islands in the South Pacific.

According to Daniken, the stone carvings on this Mayan gravestone show a spaceman in a rocket.

There are indeed many unsolved mysteries in our past. We don't necessarily need extraterrestrials in order to explain them, however. On closer examination we find that Daniken's theories have little basis in fact, and that many of his "mysteries" are not really mysteries at all. The "space helmets," for example, are depictions of animal masks with horns. Such masks were used in hunting ceremonies. We now know that space travelers don't need large antennas on their helmets anyway. Experiments show that great stone structures can be built with simple means. There are even paintings on the walls of Egyptian temples that show the construction process — but no sign of extraterrestrial help. Besides, many of the gigantic stone structures Daniken claims were built in the distant past aren't really very old. The cities of the Aztecs were built in the 14th century. The newest of the 40-foot-high stone heads on the Easter Islands was carved around 1600 — about 100 years after the discovery of America!

The huge lines in the ground at Nazca aren't much older. For some reason, Indians removed the dark upper layer of stone, exposing the layer of light sand underneath. Sand doesn't make a good runway, however. Taking myths as proof of the existence of extraterrestrials is like using "Hansel and Gretel" to prove that witches once built gingerbread houses. These ancient myths are full of metaphors, symbols, and analogies, and it often takes years of study before we can understand them. And the stone drawing of the Mayan priest in Palenque? It is a gravestone, and if you look closely you can see that the "spacecraft" is actually a corn stalk!

Are Daniken's claims plausible?

ASSISTANCE FROM EXTRATERRESTRIALS?
According to Daniken the colossal stone statues on the Easter Islands could only have been carved and set up by more advanced extraterrestrials. The Norwegian researcher Thor Heyerdahl proved that this is not the case. In an experiment, he got the inhabitants of the island to produce a new statue like the old ones. They were able to do so using chisels to carve the rock and they then managed to stand it up using only a dozen workers.

Mysteries of the Past

NO ONE KNOWS where Atlantis was located or even if there really was such a place. Some claim it was located in the Atlantic, others say it was not. People have claimed it was in the Bermuda Triangle, or that it was on the island of Helgoland, in the Sahara, in Holland, on the Ukrainian peninsula of Crimea, in Spain, on Sri Lanka, in Spitsbergen, or in about 50 other places. The theory that a city on the Mediterranean Island of Santorini was the model for Atlantis is more probable. Santorini was destroyed by a volcanic eruption in around 1650 BC.

The philosopher Plato (427–347 BC) wrote that there was once a great island called Atlantis that lay in the Atlantic Ocean beyond the "Pillars of Hercules" (that is what they called the Strait of Gibraltar between Africa and Spain in ancient times). He based his claim on the ancient stories of Egyptian priests.

Did Atlantis actually exist?

Atlantis, he said, was fertile, rich in fragrant plants and animals of all kinds, and had great mineral resources. The capital, lay at the edge of a broad, artificially irrigated plain, and at its center was the magnificent palace of the king. It was encircled by three concentric canals with bridges. A covered canal branching of from the circular canals connected them with the ocean. There were also gigantic walls encircling the city, which were covered with a shining metal. The inhabitants of Atlantis were great seafarers and warriors but when they attacked the city of

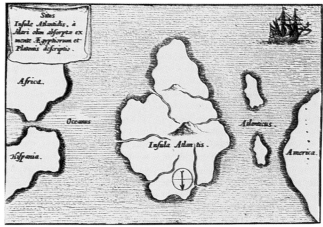

In the 17th century some thought that the island of Atlantis was located in the ocean between Gibraltar and America.

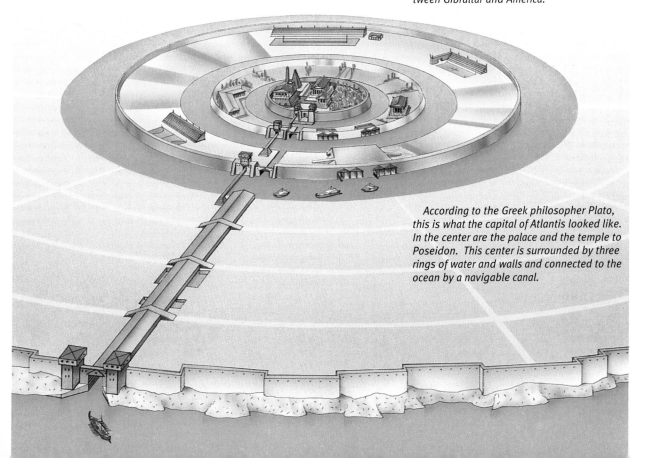

According to the Greek philosopher Plato, this is what the capital of Atlantis looked like. In the center are the palace and the temple to Poseidon. This center is surrounded by three rings of water and walls and connected to the ocean by a navigable canal.

Athens, the Greeks defeated them. Soon after, a time of great catastrophes began. The earth began to quake and the ocean washed over the land, and in one terrible day and night the entire island of Atlantis sank into the sea. According to the Egyptian priests, this had happened 9,000 years before their time. From our point in time — considering the fact that Plato lived some 2,350 years ago — this would be about 11,500 years ago.

Many people consider the question of Atlantis' existence to be one of the great mysteries of human history. For centuries Plato's story has stimulated our imaginations. Even in ancient times there was doubt about the truth of the story, however. Many authors argued that all Plato wanted to do in his (unfinished or partially preserved) text was to give us a blueprint for an ideal state. But his report is astonishingly rich in detail — the width of the canals, the size of the fertile plain, the number of war chariots and horses — everything is itemized exactly.

More than 5,000 books have been written about Atlantis and almost all of the authors consider Plato's story to be true. The most significant interpretation of the tale of Atlantis, "Atlantis, the Antediluvian World," was written by American diplomat

ATLANTIS IS NOT THE ONLY PLACE IN LEGEND that sank into the ocean. The city of Vineta was supposedly located on the Baltic coast of Germany, and the Kingdom of Lyonesse off Cornwall in England. Legend reports that an entire continent in the Indian Ocean — Lemuria — sank into the sea!

Ignatius Donnelly in 1882. In his book Donnelly paints a picture of a large, rich island in the middle of the Atlantic Ocean where the first advanced civilization on Earth flourished. Long before other cultures Atlantis was using metals and had developed writing, the compass, navigation, gunpowder, paper, and astronomy. Later authors adopted these ideas and developed them further: in their accounts Atlantis becomes a technologically advanced civilization whose knowledge surpassed our own and which had even developed space travel, atomic energy, and extrasensory perception. The authors claim that the people of Atlantis passed a part of this knowledge on to other highly developed civilizations like the Egyptians in the Old World and the Mayans and Aztecs in the Americas.

The dates cause a problem, however. 12,000 years ago neither Egypt nor Athens existed, and both play a large role in Plato's account. At that time the Ice Age was just ending. Very early on researchers thought that the Egyptian priests could have meant

This is the view travelers might have seen if they approached Atlantis by sea.

months and not years. That would place the disappearance of Atlantis at 1359 BC. However, according to geological research, there was no large island in the Atlantic at that time that would even have come close to fitting Plato's description. Thus the riddle of Atlantis remains unsolved.

There are many indications that we have long underestimated the intelligence and knowledge of our ancestors.

Is Stonehenge a prehistoric observatory?

One of the many examples of their accomplishments is Stonehenge, a massive circle of stones in southern England. It was built about 2,800 BC. Its most striking feature is the horseshoe-shaped formation made of five gigantic "trilithons" (a Greek word meaning "formation of 3 stones").

One of the trilithons at Stonehenge. These "tri-stones" are aligned according to the rising and setting of the Sun and Moon on the first day of spring and on the first day of summer.

Each trilithon is made up of two upright stones, each over 23 feet high and weighing 50 tons — as much as 40 mid-sized cars. An enormous stone crossbeam (lintel) rests atop each pair. This horseshoe is surrounded by other stone circles like the "Sarsen circle," which is made of 30 blocks, each 13 feet high and weighing 25 tons. Originally there were also 7-ton crossbeams resting atop these stones as well. An earthen wall 330 feet in diameter surrounds the whole formation.

The transport and the erection of these massive stones is an incredible technical achievement by itself. The large blocks come from a quarry 19 miles away! The most amazing thing about Stonehenge, however, is not so much the stones themselves as their arrangement. Computer calculations in recent years have shown that the formation is actually an enormous observatory for studying the paths of the Sun and Moon. The stones are set up to mark imaginary lines pointing to the places on the horizon where the Sun will rise at the summer and winter solstices (the

Were the massive stone circles of Stonehenge a prehistoric observatory? The stones are arranged according to movements of the Sun and Moon.

STONEHENGE and many similar stone circles in England and elsewhere have given rise to many stories. Some say that witches or druids — Celtic priests — once held their gatherings there. Others say that mysterious powers radiate from the stones. Still others claim that the stone circles are part of a network of "lines of power" stretching over the whole country. There is no evidence to support these claims.

ANCIENT TECHNOLOGY was probably much more advanced than we tend to believe. The Romans already used lawnmowers, greenhouses, elevators, odometers (for measuring distances traveled), airbeds, concrete, and dentures. In ancient China they already had seismometers, pipelines, deep drilling (using bamboo pipes), compasses, paper, aluminum alloys, smallpox vaccinations, and dental fillings. Europeans first made porcelain in the 18th century; the Chinese were already producing it in the 7th century AD — which is why we often call it "china."

longest and shortest days of the year) and where the Moon will appear at certain times of the year. Similar ancient observation sites have been found in North America and in Mayan settlements in Central America. The Egyptian pyramids and many of the Nazca lines in Peru are also oriented to the four points of the compass. Apparently our ancestors already had amazingly thorough knowledge of the stars thousands of years ago.

Around 1900, fishermen discovered an instrument near the island of Antikythera north of Crete that shows that our ancestors had advanced astronomical and mechanical skills. In a 2,000-year-old shipwreck they found some calcified lumps that seemed to contain something made of bronze. Not until archaeologists cleaned them and found letters, calibration marks, and cogwheels did they re-

Was the "machine of Antikythera" an ancient computer?

alized that this discovery was something extraordinary.

After lengthy detective work that began in 1951, an American researcher finally solved the puzzle. The discovery turned out to be one of the great archaeological sensations of all times. It was a kind of mechanical computer, driven by a crank and showing the times of sunrise, the phases of the Moon, the equinox, and the movements of the five planets known at that time. From the machine's settings archaeologists could tell it was built around 87 BC, probably on the Mediterranean island of Rhodes. Archaeologists knew the Greeks were already using cogwheels at least 200 years before this. They found something even more interesting in the machine, however — a differential gear, one of the most complicated mechanical elements there is. In modern times it was first patented in 1828 and is now part of every car. The real inventor was evidently a mechanic on the island of Rhodes — almost 2,000 years earlier.

An artist's reconstruction of the 2,000-year-old machine of Antikythera, a kind of mechanical astro-computer.

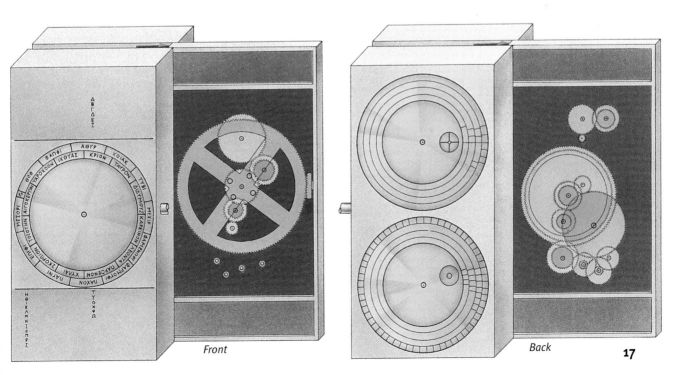

Front

Back

17

In 1936, Wilhelm König, a German researcher working at the archaeological museum in Baghdad, Iraq, noticed an unusual object. It came from the ruins of the Parthian settlement Chujat Rabuah, near Baghdad. The Parthians ruled the Tigris and Euphrates basin from about 247 BC until 224 AD. At first glance the find did not seem unusual — just a six-inch-tall clay vase. In the vase was a copper cylinder and in the cylinder was a rusted iron rod. There were traces of lead on the end of the rod sticking out of the vase. The pieces were joined together with bitumen, a tar-like substance that occurs naturally in that region. König examined the strange object and suddenly realized what he was holding: the remains of an electric battery! Apparently the Parthians discovered electric current almost 2,000 years before Luigi Galvani and Alessandro Volta, who lived about 200 years ago and until now were considered the inventors of the battery.

Of course people questioned König's findings. They sounded improbable. But a German Egyptologist, Dr. Arne Eggebrecht, built a replica, attached a gauge to it, and filled the clay vase with vinegar. Immediately the gauge registered 0.5 volts. The Parthians, he said, probably used the electricity for applying a fine, even layer of gold on small figures. However, other scientists suggested the vase was a small case for sacred writings that were rolled up on the iron rod.

This clay vase contains an iron rod and a copper cylinder. Is it possible that people had electric batteries 2,000 years ago?

There are still unanswered questions, however. How did the Parthians discover electrical current? Voltage under a half a volt cannot be measured without a gauge. Even the smallest flashlight is three times as strong. Galvani's discovery 1,800 years later was pure coincidence. He noticed that frog's legs twitched from an "electric shock" when touched by two different metals at the same time. Did the Parthians also discover electricity by accident? How did they know about connecting wires? How did they discover that you could cause dissolved gold to precipitate out of a solution by running electric current through it? Were other peoples also familiar with this invention, which seems to have been in use for several hundred years? We have no answers. There are no records, no further discoveries. The only evidence of this sensational 2,400-year-old invention is this single, unassuming museum piece.

The few findings from those times that we have stumbled upon demonstrate the high level of knowledge the artisans, chemists,

HOW DID EGGEBRECHT figure out what these batteries were used for? He had a small statue of the Egyptian god Osiris, from around 400 BC. It was made of silver and covered with an unusually thin layer of gold. He had often wondered how the artist managed to apply such a fine, even layer of gold. He hung a silver model of the figure in an aurate (gold salt) solution and connected it to a chain of ten of these clay vases. Within a few hours a thin layer of gold had formed on the model.

THE PHOENICIANS had a reputation in the ancient world as the most skilled sailors and merchants. They founded many colonies on the coasts and islands of the Mediterranean — in Africa and Spain, and on Sicily and Malta, for example. The city of Carthage, in what is now Tunisia, was the most important of these colonies. Even after Alexander the Great destroyed Phoenicia's leading city, Tyre, in 332 BC, Carthage remained a major force in the Mediterranean. Until Rome destroyed it in 146 BC, Carthage was Rome's most significant maritime rival in the Mediterranean.

and metalworkers of those times had. Who knows what else we might discover?

Many things are probably lost forever. Some of the inventions were not known to the public — they were kept secret. And of all of the literature of ancient times only a small fraction has been preserved and is available to us today. Most was lost to the fortunes of war, to great fires, and in the unrest after the collapse of the Roman Empire.

What did ancient civilizations know about the Earth?

There is nothing more than a brief reference in the writings of the Greek historian Herodotus (approx. 490-425 BC) to remind us of one of the greatest voyages of discovery in the ancient world. Around 600 BC several ships sailed around Africa (called Libya at that time). "We know that Libya is surrounded by water on all sides ex-

The Phoenicians were well-known seafarers. This stone carving from 9 BC shows a Phoenician ship. Among other things, they traveled around Africa on one of their expeditions. During this expedition they noticed that the noontime sun was in the north when seen from the southern part of Africa. This surprised them since, in the Mediterranean, it is always in the south at noon.

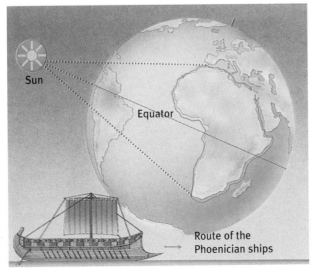

Sun

Equator

Route of the Phoenician ships

cept where it is joined to Asia. Pharaoh Necos made this discovery. He sent a number of ships manned by Phoenicians to sail to the Pillars of Hercules (Strait of Gibraltar) and return by way of the Mediterranean Sea. The Phoenicians sailed from the Red Sea out into the Indian Ocean. When autumn came, they went on land on the spot they happened to be at that moment. They planted grain and waited until they could harvest it. After the harvest they set sail again. Thus two whole years passed and it was not until the third year that they passed through the Pillars of Hercules and completed their homeward journey. Once at home they reported that as they sailed around Libya they had the Sun on their right, which some may believe, though I myself do not."

What Herodotus could not believe is actually the greatest proof that the story was true. Indeed, for seafarers south of the equator the Sun is in the north at midday — travelling west it would be on their right. In their wooden boats these seafarers covered over 15,000 miles in uncharted waters!

Phoenicians and Carthaginians were considered the best sailors of the ancient world and that is why Pharaoh Necos drew on their knowledge. They were traders and opened new trade routes during their voyages of exploration — to the tin mines of Britain, for example. Starting at Carthage in 530 BC, the Phoenician Hanno led an expedition along the west coast of Africa, probably reaching what is now known as Cameroon.

The ancient Greeks were also very interested in strange new lands. The geographer Eratosthenes (273 to 192 BC) not only wrote a detailed work about the regions of the Earth (unfortunately only parts of it survive today), he also came quite close in calculating the circumference of the Earth. He believed that you could reach India by sailing continually west — something that Columbus attempted 1,700 years later!

About 330 BC the sailor and astronomer Pytheas left the Greek colony of Massila (Marseilles, France today) on an expedition north to the tin islands where the raw material for making bronze (a copper-tin alloy) was found. He traveled through the Rhone and Loire River valleys to the Atlantic coast. There he boarded a ship and sailed to the tin mines of Cornwall on the southwest tip of England. He then sailed up the west coast of England and visited Ireland, the Hebrides, and the Orkney Islands. Traveling further north, he sailed around the main island of Britain, correctly recording its shape as triangular. He then made a detour to the north during which he presumably reached the Norwegian coast near Trondheim and, on the return trip, the island of Helgoland, known for its amber deposits.

Later authors attacked Pytheas and called him a liar. His stories were too fantastic. He claimed that in the north the sea had solidified and seemed to be covered with jellyfish (he probably saw ice floes). He said that during the summer the Sun never set there, and also that the sea breathed in a six-hour rhythm, caused by the Moon — tides, in other words (which do not occur in the Mediterranean). Only fragments of Pytheas' report survived but they are enough to demonstrate that he was one of the most important astronomers, geographers, and explorers of ancient times.

This ancient Phoenician silver coin shows a galley with its many rowers — and a seahorse.

IF PYTHEAS had not provoked disbelief among his contemporaries we would probably never have known about his astonishing journey. His report of the journey has not survived to our times, but the criticisms and mockery of other authors did survive and we can still read them today. What we know of his remarkable journey has been pieced together from quotations in these sources.

EARLY SEAFARERS

It would be a mistake to think that only Europeans undertook great sea voyages. When European ships first reached the scattered islands of the Pacific they found them settled by people who had long ago sailed thousands of miles across the open ocean in canoes, guided only by the stars. They even had maps of the Pacific and its islands — made of sticks and shells. On all of the islands there were villages and cultivated fields, and on some there were even ancient cobblestone roads, gigantic stone statues, and pyramids.

Did people from the "Old World" visit the Americas in ancient times?

The Americas may not have been unknown to some peoples in the ancient world — the Carthaginians for example. Their contemporaries considered them daring and secretive, and they were certainly familiar with the Atlantic Ocean. Some scholars have even suggested that they reached the Americas. So far, however, there is no convincing proof. Who knows, however, what secret books and maps were lost when the Romans burned Carthage in 146 BC.

The Norwegian explorer Thor Heyerdahl (born 1914) has long believed that explorers traveled to other continents thousands of years ago. The oceans and their currents, he said, were no barrier for these seafaring peoples but rather a kind of road between the continents. We know, for example, that thousands of years ago the Polynesians settled almost all of the islands of the Pacific with simple open boats. There are also theories that say Chinese and Japanese expeditions once landed on the west coast of the Americas. Of course it is difficult to prove such claims. Even if these travelers left behind objects unique to their cultures, these objects wouldn't have survived the ravages of time.

Heyerdahl was not afraid to do what it took to prove his theories — even if it involved some danger. In 1947 he built a primitive wooden raft and drifted 4,800 miles across the Pacific to prove that people from South America could have settled the South Sea Islands. Later, in 1970, he traveled across the Atlantic in a reed boat, following routes prehistoric seafarers might have followed in similar reed boats thousands of years before Columbus landed in the New World.

The Norwegian explorer Thor Heyerdahl crossed the Pacific in this balsa wood raft in 1947. He wanted to prove that prehistoric contact between South America and the South Sea Islands was possible.

In recent years we have found indications that the ancient world knew about — and mapped — more of the world than we had previously thought. This knowledge was collected and recorded by seafarers whose names were forgotten long ago. Their maps did not survive into our times, however. This is hardly surprising. These maps and the valuable information they contained — about foreign lands and trade routes — were state secrets. They were kept locked up in archives so that competitors — other traders or military officers from foreign lands — could not get at the valuable information. In addition, the maps were drawn on papyrus (a type of paper) or parchment (tanned animal skins) or a similar perishable material. There were also very few copies since only a few people were supposed to have access to the documents and maps.

It seems, however, that parts of some ancient maps did survive until modern times, at least until the beginning of the 16th century. In 1929 part of a world map was discovered in the old library of the Sultan's palace in Istanbul, Turkey. The fragment was approximately 400 years old and contained details that puzzle researchers to this day. Piri Reis, an admiral of the Ottoman fleet, drew it around 1513. He claimed he had used 20 older maps in preparing his version. Istanbul — or Constantinople as it was once called — was the center of the Eastern Roman Empire from ancient times until 1453 AD. Given this history, it is possible that a great deal of ancient wisdom was preserved there.

The American historian Charles H. Hapgood began studying the Piri Reis map in 1956. He transferred the unusual map system onto the modern grid of latitude and longitude and was able to show mistakes that Piri Reis had made in copying the older maps — after all, the admiral did not know most of the places on his map personally. For example, the Amazon is drawn twice because Reis evidently did not realize that the two large rivers on two of the original maps were one and the same. In examining the map Hapgood discovered an amazing accuracy in Reis' charting of parts of South America that he could hardly have known in 1513. After all, this was only 20 years after Columbus' first voyage and the discovery of the continent!

Columbus landed on an island in the Caribbean in 1492. Since then we have honored him as the discoverer of the Americas. In reality, sailors representing various peoples reached the "New World" long before him.

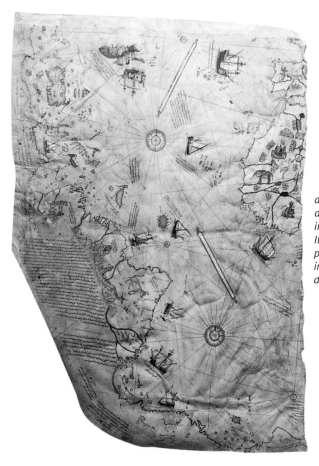

The Turkish admiral Piri Reis drew this map in about 1513. It even shows parts of America in astonishing detail.

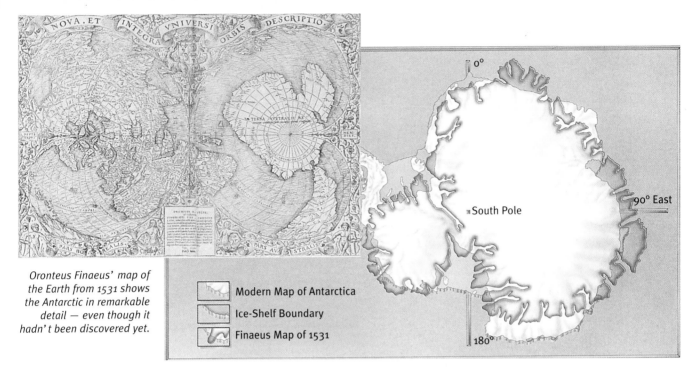

Oronteus Finaeus' map of the Earth from 1531 shows the Antarctic in remarkable detail — even though it hadn't been discovered yet.

Modern Map of Antarctica
Ice-Shelf Boundary
Finaeus Map of 1531

0°

South Pole

90° East

180°

COLUMBUS didn't just sail into the blue when he made his voyages of discovery. He consulted a map of the Atlantic on which many newly discovered islands were shown. This map was a fanciful representation of the Atlantic Ocean. The cartographer had fabricated a series of islands with names such as "Haiti-Zipango" and "Antilla." Unfortunately this document has been lost and we only know it existed because Columbus mentioned it in his diaries. There are indications that this map was one of twenty maps that Piri Reis used as a basis for his map. The fragment of Piri Reis' map may give us an idea of what Columbus' map looked like.

What is also interesting is that the Turkish admiral showed the Antarctic on his map — connected to the southern tip of South America, however. The sixth continent is shown even more accurately on a map made in 1531 by the French mapmaker Oronteus Finaeus. If you compare Piri Reis' map to a present-day one you will immediately notice an amazing similarity. Even the form of the western Antarctic is recognizable — only the Antarctic Peninsula is missing. And this map was drawn about 250 years before the modern discovery of the sixth continent! Captain James Cook, who discovered the Antarctic in 1773, had to struggle against storms, ice, and fog and never actually set foot on the continent. According to climate researchers, the situation was not much different in the thousands of years before his visit. How is it possible that seafarers were able to reach the continent long before Cook and to record the outline of the coast on their maps? We do know that mapmakers of

that time often drew a fictional southern continent for the sake of symmetry between northern and southern hemispheres. If this is all he was doing when he added an additional continent at the tip of South America, then Piri Reis was astonishingly lucky with his fiction.

Hapgood, who also examined the Finaeus map, believes that these maps were based on very old maps drawn up in a warmer period before the Antarctic was covered by ice. He believes there were other highly developed civilizations on Earth before those known to us (like the Egyptians, the Sumerians, and the Chinese) who have long since been forgotten. This wouldn't explain why only the maps of these ancient civilizations have survived, however, and no stone ruins.

Nevertheless, the similarities between the old maps and the real land masses are so great that we can no longer believe it is pure coincidence. The mystery remains — who discovered the Antarctic so long ago?

Looking Into the Future

Thousands of years ago the nighttime sky had a much greater importance for people than it does today. They saw

Where did astrology originate?

the starry sky as an image of the earthly world and placed familiar objects, legendary figures, and above all animals in the heavens. In certain groups of bright stars they saw a bull and a ram, fish and a goat, and many other images.

At the same time they were interested even more in the processes they say occurring in the sky. They observed the regular changes in the Moon; they noticed that some particularly bright stars moved differently than the others — the "wandering stars" or planets — and they contemplated what these curious spectacles might mean. Were the Sun, the Moon, and the planets perhaps gods who moved across the heavens high above them, forever beyond their reach?

THE ENGLISH PLAYWRIGHT William Shakespeare (1564–1616) was critical of astrology: "This is the excellent foppery of the world, that, when we are sick in fortune, often the surfeits of our own behavior, we make guilty of our disasters the sun, the moon, and the stars; as if we were villains on necessity; fools by heavenly compulsion ... An admirable evasion of whoremaster man, to lay his goatish disposition on the charge of a star!" (King Lear)

The constellation we call "The Seven Sisters" or "Pleiades."

Can we read our destinies in the stars? For centuries astrologers have looked for connections between celestial and earthly events.

WHAT ARE THE SIGNS OF THE ZODIAC?

If we could travel away from the Earth, we would find that the constellations of the Zodiac no longer look like they do from Earth. This is because the stars in them are all at different distances from Earth. The patterns that we attribute to the stars are limited to our viewpoint here on Earth. Even the patterns we see here are far from clear — different peoples have grouped the stars into very different patterns or constellations.

Or was this the gods' way of communicating their wishes and warnings to humans? The ancient Egyptians had long known that there was a predictable relationship between occurrences in the heavens and events on Earth. In the summer, when the bright star Sirius first appeared in the evening sky, it was a sign that the Nile would soon overflow its banks.

Astrology probably came about in a manner something like this — the belief, that is, that we can read the future in the changing arrangements of the heavenly bodies. All of the advanced cultures in Asia, Africa, and America had their stargazers, usually priests or scholars, who regularly observed the heavens, recorded what they saw, and tried to interpret it. The form of astrology practiced in our society today can be traced back to Babylonian priests. The Greeks and then the Romans adopted their practices. Even today we still use the names of Roman gods for the planets. The visible characteristics of each planet usually influenced the name it was given. Red

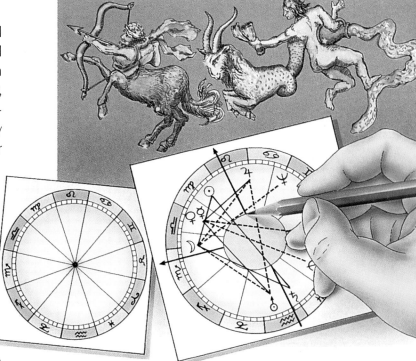

is the color of blood, so the red planet was associated with the god of war, Mars. Mercury, which moves so quickly across the sky, was given the name of the messenger of the gods. The radiantly beautiful Venus was named after the goddess of love, and the bright, serenely moving Jupiter after the father of the gods.

In the ancient world astrologers concerned themselves only with the fates of kings and empires. Rulers everywhere consulted astrologers before making decisions. Whatever it was — when to marry or go to war, when to build a palace or a ship — they asked their astrologers.

For about 2,000 years now astrologers have also been reading the future for average people. Astrologers prepare a "horoscope" in which they record the positions of the planets at the hour of your birth. Around the year 159 AD Claudius Ptolemy, a Greek living in Alexandria in Egypt, gathered all the astrological knowledge of the time in his book "Tetrabiblos." Present-day astrology still draws on the basic principles of this book.

It wasn't until the 17th century that we began to distinguish between astrology — reading the future in the stars — and astronomy — the scientific study of the stars and space. Modern science does not recognize the claims of astrology.

What does a horoscope look like?

If you go to a professional astrologer today and have your horoscope prepared and interpreted, the astrologer may use a piece of paper with a circle containing the twelve signs of the

The astrologer marks the positions of the planets at the time of your birth and then interprets them.

CAN STARS INFLUENCE CHARACTER?

Many people believe that a person's star sign influences his or her character. Those born under the sign of Libra, for example, are believed to be unreliable, Gemini can adapt easily but are talkative, Pisces are self-sacrificing but also lazy. Scientific investigations have turned up no evidence that there is any connection between star sign and character traits.

This 15th century Italian miniature shows Mars and the signs of the zodiac associated with him. He stands in full battle attire, ready to do battle, blood red.

THE MOON is our nearest neighbor in space. For this reason many people believe it has some mysterious energy that can influence our lives and fates. After all, its gravity pulls the waters of the oceans and produces the tides. Many believe that the full moon disturbs sleep and causes a rise in the rates of murders, suicides, and births. It is said to disrupt operations and affect the growth of plants and hair. Statistical evidence does not support these claims.

FALSE PREDICTIONS can inspire astrologers to be amazingly imaginative when they have to explain to their customers why their predictions didn't come true. Sometimes they claim that mysterious new planets are responsible for the error. Astrologers generally express themselves as vaguely as possible anyway, and can attribute the failure to a misunderstanding by the customer. Newspaper horoscopes are particularly vague.

zodiac: Aries the Ram, Taurus the Bull, Gemini the Twins, Cancer the Crab, Leo the Lion, Virgo the Virgin, Libra the Balance, Scorpio the Scorpion, Sagittarius the Archer, Capricorn the Goat, Aquarius the Water Bearer, and Pisces the Fishes. These are the constellations

This miniature shows Mercury and his planet together with the zodiac signs Virgo and Gemini. The wings on his feet are symbols of his quickness.

the planets pass through as they orbit the Sun. Astrologers also count the Sun and Moon as planets. This is a relic of the worldview commonly accepted up until the 16th century — that the Earth was the center of the universe and everything revolved around it.

You will also find the Earth at the center of the horoscope sheet. The twelve areas around it are called "houses." In these areas the astrologer enters the signs of the planets as they stood at the time you were born — the positions of the planets on a given day can be

found in charts ("ephemerides"). Today astrologers often use computers to calculate the positions.

Now the actual work begins — the reading. This is a complicated process and real astrologers have nothing but contempt for the stock horoscopes printed in newspapers ("Aries should think twice today before acting"). There are many factors to consider: Which planet is in which constellation? Do certain planets build groups in certain houses? Are they at a particular angle to one another?

In astrology every planet, every house, and every sign has its own meaning and there are many possible combinations that must also be considered. The Sun is said to be the "male principle" in a person, the Moon is the "female" (because it receives its light from the Sun). Mercury influences reason and travel; Venus is responsible for marriage and love; Mars stands for power, courage, and strength.

There are good reasons for doubting that stars can show us the future. Astrologers themselves admit: "The stars only make us inclined to do things, they do not force us to do them." Maybe this is why astrologers fail when they attempt to prove their art in independent tests like one done recently in Holland. The 44 astrologers who took part received the birth data of seven test subjects and were asked to prepare their horoscopes. They were also given slips of paper with character descriptions of the subjects. Now

Do the stars tell the truth?

all the astrologers had to do was to match the character descriptions with the horoscopes. A large cash prize was offered to the astrologer who matched them all correctly.

The results were disappointing. Even the best astrologer only got three of seven correct; half of the participants did not get a single one right. They also disagreed among themselves and arrived at very different character traits for the same birth data. For the organizer of the competition, the Dutch Society of Skeptics, this was admittedly no surprise — all tests so far have ended much like this.

Astronomers aren't surprised at the results either, since they believe the fundamental principles of astrology are illogical. Why should the planets and signs of the zodiac influence precisely the character traits the Greeks assigned to them over 2,000 years ago? Astrologers say this is because man was more "in touch with nature" back then. Non-believers ask why the planets Uranus, Neptune and Pluto appear in modern horoscopes. They can only be seen through a powerful telescope and were thus not discovered until after 1781. The astronomers who discovered them

also chose names at random from the world of the ancient gods. Nevertheless astrologers have given each planet the characteristics that its namesake supposedly had.

Our knowledge of biology also contradicts astrology. It has long been an accepted fact that a person's personality and character are largely determined by heredity and are already fixed at the time of conception — nine months before birth. This is reason enough to suspect that the position of the stars at a child's birth can't possibly have any influence on its character.

Reading horoscopes has always been rather complicated and hence expensive. Even poorer people were troubled

What other methods of telling the future are there?

by the uncertainty of their fate, however, and they also consulted fortune-tellers. Even if these fortune-tellers didn't ask the stars, however, it doesn't mean that they pulled their knowledge out of thin air. Over the years fortune-tellers have used everything imaginable to help them foretell the future.

Fortune-tellers use crystal balls like this to see into the future.

ASTROLOGY stems from a time when the planets still symbolized gods and when people believed that the Earth was the center of the universe. Today we know that not even the Sun is at the center of the universe, and our satellites have examined the planets from close range. In such a time, astrology seems as outdated as the magical hunting ceremonies of Stone Age peoples — even if it does use computers.

Roman fortune-tellers let a chicken peck at grain in a circle divided into fields containing letters. The chicken thus "picked" certain letters and the fortune-tellers based their predictions on these letters.

CAN ANIMALS PREDICT EARTHQUAKES?

There have been many reports of strange animal behavior before earthquakes. Cats run out of the house, horses and cattle refuse to enter a barn, animals living underground unexpectedly come to the surface. Do they feel faint warning movements of Earth or sense escaping ground gases? Often there is no warning. In China some people successfully predicted an earthquake in 1970 by observing the behavior of animals. During another earthquake in 1976, however, there were no signs of danger and the quake killed 655,000 people.

Every fortune-teller — even today — has his or her specialty.

Among the Etruscans and the Romans there were special priests, the augurs, who interpreted the will of the gods — and thus the future — by reading the entrails of freshly slaughtered animals. They examined the heart and kidneys, the intestines and lungs. They paid particular attention to the liver since the liver — and not the heart — was considered the seat of life. In old graves archaeologists have found bronze models of livers that are divided into zones. Each zone had a specific significance and was assigned to a certain god.

The Romans also thought the will of the gods was revealed in the flight of certain birds, like the eagle, and in the calls of crows, owls, and ravens. The augurs also observed the way sacred chickens picked at grain, the behavior of spiders and insects, the color and movement of mice, cracks in the shoulder blades of burned animals, patterns in the ashes of burnt offerings, and even figures they saw in puddles of spilled wine. They used their observations in telling the future.

Many peoples considered fire to be holy and for this reason they

Around 5,000 years ago Sumerian fortune-tellers used this clay model of a sheep's liver for predicting the future.

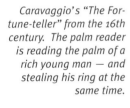

Caravaggio's "The Fortune-teller" from the 16th century. The palm reader is reading the palm of a rich young man — and stealing his ring at the same time.

Telling the future with colorful and mysterious Tarot cards. The position of the individual cards is particularly important.

A Tarot deck consists of 78 cards, each loaded with significant symbols, meanings, and repercussions for other cards, depending on the way they are laid. Some of the patterns for laying cards have names like "star" or "tree of life." Twenty-two of the cards are especially important. They have impressive names like "The Magician," "The Fool," "The Hanged Man," "Death," "The Lovers," "Judgment," and "Strength." After long study of the art of Tarot — and with a keen sense for the customer's secret wishes and thoughts — a fortune-teller is able to tell the future from the way the cards lie and the contexts in which they appear.

THE I CHING is an ancient Chinese method of fortune-telling based on "The Book of Changes." By manipulating yarrow stocks or throwing coins onto the ground, fortune-tellers determine which of the 64 hexagrams (images made up of 6 lines) in "The Book of Changes" they should consult. Each hexagram is associated with one or more rather cryptic poetic passages that fortune-tellers then use to formulate a prediction.

watched it as a mirror of fate. How does it burn? Does it give off sparks? What images do the flames and the smoke form?

The future is also reflected in human beings themselves. Man literally holds his own future in the palm of his hands — at least that is what palm readers have believed for over 4,000 years now. Lines in the palm of the hand, the shape and color of the hand, fingers, and nails all hold clues for someone who knows how to interpret them.

With the advent of printing, playing cards became inexpensive and have been very popular with fortune-tellers ever since. There has always been an air of mystery about the exotic images on Tarot cards. Some people say these pictures go back to ancient traditions. In any case they have been around at least since the end of the 14th century and are probably the forerunners of modern playing cards.

At Delphi the Pythia received "oracles" or answers from the god Apollo. Priests then interpreted the oracles for the questioners. In doing so they often influenced the politics of the time.

DELPHIC PROPHECIES were usually formulated in obscure and ambiguous language that had to be interpreted for the questioner by a priest. This is true of prophecies today: fortune-tellers always use an ambiguous medium. It may be a complicated horoscope, patterns in coffee grounds, combinations of cards, the tangle of lines on a hand, or the chance shapes formed by molten lead when poured into water. This gives the fortune-teller great freedom when "reading" and makes it difficult to prove the reading wrong.

How did the Oracle at Delphi work?

Fortune-tellers can make a great deal of money and gain a great deal of power. Nowhere is this more evident than in the case of the Delphic Oracle. It was the most famous center of fortune-telling in the ancient world. The city of Delphi lies at the foot of Mount Parnassus in Greece, and ancient Greeks believed it was the center or "navel" of the world. The temple at this sacred site was dedicated to the god Apollo. According to tradition, there was a priestess in the temple, the Pythia, who delivered messages from

Today there are only ruins of the temple complex at Delphi. In this picture you can see the ruins of the theater, the temple to Apollo, and the treasury.

Apollo. In an outer room, those seeking advice paid a fee and asked their questions. The questions were directed to Apollo but the answers came from the mouth of the Pythia — not in any clear language, however, but as stuttering, stammering, or screaming. Priests then interpreted the sounds for the questioner.

The Delphic Oracle functioned successfully for many centuries and became very wealthy. It wasn't until the advent of Christianity that this "heathen" rite came to an end. In 357 Emperor Constantine abolished all oracles.

No one knows how the priests at Delphi got their information since their workings were extremely secretive. There are indications that they had a network of agents and spies. In any case, while the questioners waited for their turn — they often had to wait several days — they probably passed on important information while talking to others waiting. Certainly the priests were also familiar with the political situations, power struggles, laws, and customs of surrounding lands. They may have had a kind of customer file, an an-

cient data bank where they recorded the information they gathered.

The oracle was famous for ambiguous answers. For example, when King Croesus asked if he should risk going to war against the Persians, he was told, "If you cross the Halys," — the river that formed the border between the two countries — "you will destroy a great empire." Croesus took this to mean he would defeat the Persians — and was defeated himself. The great empire that he destroyed was his own! Either way, however, the Oracle would have been right.

Of course the priests profited from their customers' tendency to praise successful predictions and to blame themselves when the predictions did not come true.

The French physician and astrologer Nostradamus wrote hundreds of cryptic verses in the mid-16th century. He still has many followers today.

Who was Nostradamus?

One of the great masters of the art of hiding prophecy in puzzling sayings was the Frenchman Michel de Notredame, who used the Latin name Nostradamus. He lived from 1503 to 1566 in the Provence in southern France where he practiced medicine. One of his hobbies was astrology and he claimed to have "fits" of prophetic wisdom. He presented his revelations in 952 poems of four lines each. They are short, incomplete sentences in an old form of French, mixed with bits and pieces of Latin and the dialect of the Provence. He published them in 1555 and in 1558. They were already difficult for people of that time to understand, not to mention for the present-day French. Still, his prophecies, which suppos-

edly reach into the year 3790, brought him not only scorn and derision, but also fame. He is considered the best known fortune-teller in the world.

Few of his verses include a date, however, and on the dates he does mention — 1580, 1607, 1609, 1700, 1703, and 1727 — nothing happened that came even close to what the passages for those dates described. Nevertheless his followers maintain that his verses predicted the French Revolution, Hitler, World War II, the end of the papacy, and in general a great deal of murder, violence, blood, and crime.

Naturally, the followers of Nostradamus did not discover the meaning of his texts until after the fact. Or more precisely: among the thousand odd poems, they found at least one that more or less fit the events.

THE FORTUNE-TELLER'S GIFT lies in keen observation and an ability to empathize with the client's worries and desires. Behavior, clothing, and body language tell us a lot about people. The fortune-teller can draw conclusions through careful questioning and close observation of the client's reactions. Besides, most people hear what they want to hear and would like to believe — not what is really said.

Forces From the Hereafter

WHICH COUNTRY HAS THE MOST GHOSTS?

Britain is often considered to be prime real estate for ghosts. When author Diane Norman was researching a book on English ghosts she wrote to the owners of 30 of the oldest castles and estates in England to ask whether their buildings were haunted. She received 28 positive answers.

Where can you find ghosts?

During the daylight hours swarms of tourists wander through the old halls of the "Tower" in London. They visit the armory with its suits of armor, swords, and shields and stand in awe in front of the glittering crown jewels and dazzling jewelry in the Vault. But at night the halls and stairways of the centuries-old castle sink into a silence broken only by the guards making their regular rounds. Sometimes, they claim, they see a strange human-like form with blurred outlines that silently floats by, bathed in an eerie white light. The figure appears especially on cold, gloomy nights, and upon closer examination, they say, you can see that it is a woman in a magnificent gown — holding her head under her right arm!

This, they claim, is the ghost of Ann Boleyn. She was the second wife of the English king, Henry the Eighth and the mother of the famous Queen Elisabeth I. When her royal husband got tired of her, he had her placed in the Tower under false accusations and then beheaded in 1536. To this day her soul has found no rest.

In England there is nothing unusual about contact with ghosts. The British Isles — England, Scotland, and Ireland — are well-known for their numerous haunted castles and bewitched houses.

The ruins of Rathpeak House in the Irish country of Roscommon are said to be haunted by the spirit of a young woman whose broth-

The Tower of London by night. The ghost of Anne Boleyn is said to roam its halls.

Are we influenced by powers from the hereafter? Séances and reports of ghosts suggest that many people believe we are.

PEOPLE AREN'T the only ones who can haunt. There are also many reports of animals that suddenly and inexplicably appear: dogs that have long been dead, cats that have just drowned, and horses that fell in battle. Some people even tell of seeing buildings long after they have been torn down or destroyed. In 1854 in Westphalia, Germany several people claimed they saw a phantom battle.

coins across the room, turned liquids into ink, knocked on things to call attention to herself, and made things disappear mysteriously. A fire broke out in 1939 and the house burned to the ground. Now the "spookiest" house in England is the manor house "Sanford Orcas" in the county of Dorset. The owner reports having 14 different ghosts, among them a black hunting dog.

er buried her alive behind the wall of their house. He did so because she fell in love with a man of another religion.

Glamis Castle, near the city of Dundee, Scotland, was built in the 13th century. In the autumn fog it looks like the perfect haunted castle — with its many turrets and spires. According to the local people, a monster steals through the rooms of the castle — half man, half animal. The ghost of the "Gray Lady" haunts the castle chapel — some say it is Lady Glamis, who was burned at the stake as a witch in 1540.

One of the most famous haunted houses was the Borley Rectory in the county of Essex — it was considered "the most uncanny house in all of England." For decades, it is said, a nun worked her mischief there as a "Poltergeist." She didn't usually appear in a visible form, but rather threw bowls, stones, or

What are ghosts?

The belief in ghosts is an old phenomenon that can be found worldwide. The Roman writer Pliny the Younger, who died in 113 AD, wrote of a ghostly figure that wandered through a house in chains and then disappeared into the floor. When they dug at the site, they found a skeleton bound in chains.

The Chinese distinguish between "shen," the good and hon-

The cellar of Glamis Castle in Scotland. Some say that on foggy autumn nights a monster that is half man and half animal haunts the castle.

The Englishman John Dee (1527–1608) was a very famous astrologer. He often worked together with a controversial medium named Edward Kelly.

person. This belief is very old and can be found in many religions. Traditional Christianity, for example, teaches that the soul goes to heaven or hell after death. If this is so, then it is certainly possible that the souls of the dead do not go directly to their destination, but must wait for a while in some realm in between, in a "limbo." In certain cases, especially if they met a violent

orable spirits of one's ancestors, and "kuei," the evil spirits of darkness, who bring misfortune. The ugliest ghosts are probably the Japanese ones, who haunt cemeteries or old houses — they have mutilated arms and legs, misshapen bodies, and sometimes severe wounds.

Not all ghost stories tell about ghosts that haunt one specific house or place over centuries. Sometimes a dying person's spirit appears to friends or close relatives at the moment of death, or a given spirit appears whenever a death or tragedy is about to happen.

The belief in spirits is closely tied to the belief that a person lives on after death in some form or another — if not in body, then at least in spirit: the thoughts and feelings, the wishes and hopes of a

A MODERN FORM OF GHOST is the "hitch-hiking ghost." A driver picks up a girl in his car and they have a pleasant conversation, but the girl suddenly disappears when they reach their destination. The driver then learns that the girl was hit by a car and killed — shortly before he picked her up.

The "Flying Dutchman" allegedly sails with a crew of ghosts, damned to sail forever. Superstitious sailors believed its appearance was a sign of impending doom.

death, they may even remain tied to the world of the living.

Some people claim that there are entire ship's crews that sail the oceans like this on ghost ships, damned to sail for eternity and never find rest. The most famous of these tales is that of the "Flying Dutchman." According to the legend he cursed God and has been sailing aimlessly through the southern Atlantic near the Cape of Good Hope since 1641. Woe to the ship that meets such a ghostly sailor — it is doomed to sink.

How do mediums try to contact the dead?

In about the middle of the nineteenth century so-called spiritualism came into fashion in America and Europe. With the help of a person with a special "gift" — we call such a person a "medium" — people tried to contact the spirit world and ask questions. The first docu-

mented "conversation" with a spirit took place in a haunted house near New York City on March 31, 1848. Every night the owners, the Fox family, heard strange knocking sounds. One of the daughters got up all her courage one night and called into the darkness, "Do what I do." She then clapped her hands four times. Immediately she heard four knocks. Then she asked, "Are you a person?" There was only silence. But when she said, "If you are a spirit, knock twice," she heard two knocks.

Soon after this a newspaper report about the two Fox sisters appeared in the "New York Herald Tribune." If we can believe their story, this was the first deliberate conversation with the spirit-world.

This was only the beginning of a craze. Mediums came out of nowhere and extolled their talents and spiritualistic associations were founded. It became quite the thing to hold "séances" — this is what they called their attempts to conjure up spirits with the help of a medium in order to receive messages from the spirit world.

The spirits of the dead made contact through mysterious voices, noises, or by lifting ("levitating") the table. They often knew private details about the deceased relative or loved one that know one else could possibly know. The "Ouija" board was particularly popular. The word "Ouija" is a combination of the French word "oui" and the German word "ja" — both of which mean "yes." The original Ouija "board" consisted of 38 cards laid out in a circle on the table: 26 cards with the letters of the alphabet, ten with the numbers 0-9 and the last two with the words "yes" and "no." In the middle was a glass that had been turned upside down. Today there is a special board for this purpose that has everything pre-printed on it. The people taking part sit around the table, each with his fingertips on the glass. Under the spirit's influence, the glass then moves towards one of the letters or numbers, spelling words or numbers, depending on the question asked.

Spiritualism must have met some deep-seated need in many people, otherwise it could never have become so successful. For many it was certainly a comfort to think that they could contact their deceased loved ones one last time. There were even some scientists who saw in spiritualism a new field of research with boundless possibilities.

A Navajo Indian medicine man. Many members of this tribe still follow their old religious traditions and customs today.

Among primitive tribes shamans place themselves in trances in order to make contact with the spirit-world.

How seriously can we take séances?

We now know that many of these mediums were really con-artists who took advantage of the gullibility of their fellow citizens. Many other mediums were suspected of deception, but nothing could be proven. Some actually admitted it. They usually used the simple but clever tricks of magicians. Most of the time it was not a scientist who exposed these frauds, but rather professional magicians. They even knew how to trick people under the bright light of the stage and usually performed feats that were much more amazing than anything the mediums did. The difference is that magicians do not claim to have supernatural powers.

In spite of all the swindling, some people still believe it is possible to conjure up spirits. Books on the subject still point to earlier séances that were supposedly suc-cessful, but they often fail to mention that the mediums in question have long since been exposed as fakes. Belief in the spirit-world is particularly widespread among Americans. When the University of Chicago conducted a survey a few years ago, they found that approximately 40 percent of all Americans believe they are in contact with deceased loved ones, either directly or through a medium. These mediums are called "channels" today because they allegedly create "energy channels" to the spirit-world. It has become quite fashionable to seek out channeling mediums on a regular basis.

But what do these mediums base their claims on? For years now "ghost hunters" have been trying to document the same strange phenomena that people living in haunted houses claim to have seen. Even using cameras, tape recorders, and reliable witnesses, they have not been able to provide scientific evidence for even one of the many reported hauntings. This doesn't mean that all these people deliberately lied. It is more likely that their senses deceived them, making them see things that weren't really there. Such phenomena are called hallucinations and anyone who has experienced one really does believe that what they are experiencing is real. This can happen to someone who is under emotional stress — for example when a loved one is very ill. It is often in such situations that people report having seen spirits.

Of course human gullibility is a big help. Frank Smyth, editor of the magazine "People, Myths and Magic," conducted an experiment in London in 1970 that showed just how gullible people often are. He invented a ghost together with a complete description and history, and named the place where it had been seen and "eyewitnesses" who had seen it. He then printed this story in his magazine. No one doubted the authenticity of the story and within one year references to it showed up in eight different books, often with new details added. When television reporters visited the place where it was all supposed to have happened, several people said they had seen the ghost. After the television broadcast, baskets full of letters arrived at the station with further sightings!

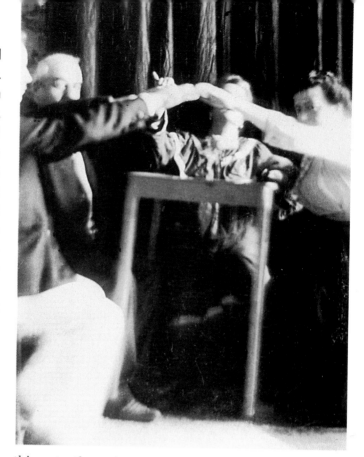

During a séance a table levitates — without any human help? There is no known explanation for this phenomenon — except in cases of obvious fraud.

What is psi?

You are thinking about someone you have not seen for a long time and all of a sudden the phone rings and that person is on the other end of the line. A thought flashes through your mind and the person you are talking to says the same thing. You concentrate on the dice wishing for a six — and you get one!

Who has not had experiences like this? For centuries people have been reporting such coincidences. What they all have in common is that the person suddenly knew or felt something that didn't come from one of their five senses — seeing, hearing, smelling, tasting, touching. This "extrasensory" ("beyond the senses") ability seems to be particularly well developed in some people. They seem to have a "sixth" sense that reveals

things to them that are far away or even in the future. For many years people thought these abilities had something to do with the devil and with spirits. Serious researchers, however, have been interested in this area for several decades. They call themselves "parapsychologists." These mysterious abilities are also called "psi phenomena," after the next-to-the-last letter of the Greek alphabet, or ESP — "extrasensory perception."

So far there is no scientifically proven way to send messages from one mind to another without using at least one of the five known senses. The same is true of seeing into the future or moving objects by "mental powers."

Of course if it could be proven that such extrasensory abilities really do exist, it would be a sensation. It would also have a great effect on our present scientific view of the world.

PSYCHIC PHOTOGRAPHS
Accidental photographs of spirits and supernatural apparitions are called psychic photographs. They supposedly only appear after the film has been developed and are invisible before this process. There are thousands of these pictures, though it is of course very easy to produce such images through double exposure or a hidden second lens.

In view of the many reports of ESP experiences, you would think it would not be difficult to get scientific evidence, for example through experiments. In reality, parapsychologists are having a difficult time, even though they have been trying for decades. There is still no proof that would convince skeptical scientists. They argue that such everyday experiences could be pure coincidence — and that coincidence generally rules our lives. When a thought and an event unexpectedly coincide, however, it certainly seems like the thought "caused" the event.

Psychologist Joseph B. Rhine was the first researcher to attempt a systematic study of these psi-

Rhine's cards

phenomena. Starting in about 1930 he tested a large number of subjects at his Parapsychological Institute in North Carolina.

For his experiments Rhine used a kind of guessing game with special cards. Each deck had 25 cards. There were five of each image —

circle, star, plus sign, square, and three wavy lines. The researcher turned over the top card from a pile that had been thoroughly shuffled. The test subject was sitting in another room and was supposed to determine which of the five pictures it was — using ESP (or by guessing). Both kept an exact record of the series of pictures and afterwards they compared notes and counted the number of correct answers.

The average results even for very talented test subjects were only slightly better than chance results. The test subjects also seemed to lose their extrasensory abilities if they were disturbed, if the tests took too long, if non-believers were present, or for a variety of other reasons. In any case, these were the reasons Rhine gave for excluding the lowest test results from his statistics. That means that only the more successful tests were counted, however, and falsified statistics such as this prove nothing — they are simply manipulation. In any case, the scientific community seriously questioned the results of Rhine's tests because of this obvious mathematical imprecision.

In the meantime other researchers have repeated these tests with the help of computers and more sophisticated testing methods in order to eliminate mistakes and frauds. Even in the best case, however, the result was still only a little better than the statistical average.

Despite these problems, parapsychologists still firmly believe that there is such a thing as psi. More critical scientists say there is

COINCIDENCE OR NOT?

The downside of methods such as Rhine's is that they require a large number of experiments in order to obtain meaningful results. As with rolling dice, where it is not unusual to roll fours sixes in a row, coincidence can also produce a number of right answers or a number of wrong answers in a row. You need thousands of correctly administered tests to obtain a reliable result.

not enough proof. If extrasensory abilities really do exist and if they can be measured with such tests, then they are extremely weak and uncertain. Have you ever heard of anyone winning the lottery more than once? It shouldn't be difficult for someone with ESP to predict the numbers a few days in advance.

Geologists were impressed. Hans Schröter, a hydraulic engineer for the German Association for Technical Cooperation,

Can dowsers find water and gold?

found water on the island of Sri Lanka 664 times in 691 attempts, although there was very little water in some cases. Only 27 times did he come up dry. What is unusual about this story, besides the fact that he was so successful, is the way Schröter found the water — with a divining rod. The control tests were even more impressive. Researchers selected two 300-foot-deep boreholes that they knew were dry. To test Schröter, they asked him to use his divining rod to look for water as close to the two holes as possible. Only 100 feet away from one of the dry holes he really did find water at a depth of only 120 feet. In the 20 years Schröter has been "dowsing" he

has been extraordinarily successful in finding water all over the world.

For many centuries people have been using the divining rod as an all-purpose instrument for finding mineral resources. With a simple forked twig they claim they can find water, gold, ore, coal, and even buried treasure. Dowsers have their individual preferences for certain kinds of twigs — hazel, cherry, etc. Actually, it doesn't even have to be a twig: modern dowsers usually use simple, L-shaped metal rods. They hold one in each hand, pointing them straight ahead, and then slowly walk forward. At the right spot the ends of the rods suddenly swing out away from each other or in toward each other. Most dowsers claim that from the force of the rod's movement they can tell the type, depth, and quality of the mineral resource and can distinguish between fresh and salt water.

MOST DOWSERS not only claim they can find water and minerals but also that they can tell the type, depth, and quality of the mineral resources from the strength and quality of the movements in their divining rod. Some claim they can differentiate between sweet water and salt water. Some even try to find criminals or the victims of avalanches with the help of a divining rod.

In this drawing from Georg Agricola's book on mining, miners are looking for ore with a divining rod. Agricola took a very skeptical view of dowsing.

This dowser is looking for water veins with the help of a forked stick. Some dowsers now use metal or plastic rods.

"THE CARPENTER EFFECT"

It is not some mysterious emanations from the ground that causes the divining rod to move, but the "Carpenter Effect." If you imagine or observe a movement, your muscles spontaneously contract and you make a similar movement — when you see someone yawn, for example. This happens to dowsers. They expect the rod to move — perhaps subconsciously or unintentionally — and so the rod really does move. The effect is named after the British psychologist William B. Carpenter who first described it in 1852.

Opinions about dowsing are divided. The dowsers themselves swear by it, but geologists are usually doubtful. Even the natural scientist, physician, and mining expert Georg Agricola (1494–1555) wrote: "The simple miner believes in the usefulness of the divining rod since the dowser sometimes finds veins of ore by accident. A true miner does not use a magic wand since he should be a serious and pious man. Since he should know and understand the things of nature, he will recognize that a divining rod is of no use. Instead, he watches for the natural signs indicating a vein of ore."

Today dowsing is still highly controversial since even acknowledged dowsers have repeatedly failed in scientific testing. In one case, researchers sent several dowsers, one after the other, out into the same field. You would expect that the divining rods would react at the same spot each time but they almost never did. Even when asked to find water flowing in pipes deep under the ground, the dowsers failed. The rods did react, however, when the dowsers already knew where the water was.

From 1986 to 1988, the German Ministry for Research commissioned two physicists from Munich (who also believed in dowsing) to carry out the most extensive test to date. In the course of three years they sent approximately 500 dowsers over test areas, sometimes outdoors, sometimes inside barns built above buried waterlines. The results were pathetic: 99 percent of those who took part missed every single time and the results of the rest were not convincing. Even Hans Schröter was successful only four times out of ten. The other six times he was nowhere close to finding water.

In any event, no one has been able to explain scientifically what makes the rod react. The general opinion, even among dowsers, is that the rod is only a pointer and that the actual instrument is the human being holding the rod. Involuntary muscle twitches cause the loosely held rods to move. Words like "earth rays" and "stimulus zones" can be found in books on the subject and those who believe in dowsing are convinced that such rays exist. These rays are even supposed to cause diseases like cancer. So far, however, no one has offered a clear picture of what these rays are. Of course, this doesn't stop enterprising con artists from selling expensive "de-sensitizing machines." They then "demonstrate" the effectiveness of your purchase with their divining rod.

Mysterious Animals

THERE HAVE ALWAYS BEEN a lot of reports about sea monsters. One of them is Nessie, the famous monster from Loch Ness in Scotland. But it is by no means the only sea monster. There have been similar reports from Loch Morar in Scotland and from Storsjön in Sweden. In North America there are supposedly 230-foot-long snake-like monsters in Lake Manitoba in Canada and Lake Champlain between New York State and Vermont. People in South America, Africa, and Asia also tell of seeing strange sea animals in lakes.

The nightmare of early sailors: an attack by the "Kraken," a giant squid. There is evidence that unknown creatures of gigantic size really do exist in the depths of the ocean.

In October 1873, the fishermen Theophile Piccot, Daniel Squires, and 12-year-old Tom Piccot experienced a living nightmare. It was a quiet autumn day and they were drifting in their boat off the coast of Newfoundland near St. John's. They had just pulled in their full fishing nets and were preparing to return home when Tom saw an unusual object floating in the water. They rowed over to what they thought was a piece of driftwood. Suddenly, tentacles as big around as a man's arm and covered with white suction cups came up out of the water, wrapped themselves around the fishing boat, and tried to pull it into the depths. Two white eyes as big as plates stared at them. With great presence of mind Tom grabbed an ax and chopped off a tentacle. The sea monster disappeared and the fishermen quickly made for shore. Their catch, a 20 foot-long piece of a tentacle, was taken to the local priest. He recognized the significance of their find and sent it to Yale University to be examined. Zoologist Addison Verrill came to the conclusion that the tentacle belonged to a giant squid at least 30 feet long. He gave it the scientific name Architeuthis.

A year before, the body of another such animal had washed ashore in the same area. Its longest tentacle was 40 feet long. The eyes of a specimen that washed ashore in 1880 were one foot in diameter.

Richard Ellis, an acknowledged expert on marine life, has investigated these and hundreds of other stories about monsters from the deep. He is convinced there are many more unknown creatures in the depths of the ocean — some of which reach gigantic sizes. Until now such stories have been written off as "sailor's yarns" but apparently such creatures really do exist.

Actually it isn't surprising that we don't know about all the creatures living in our oceans. The oceans cover two thirds of the Earth's surface and in most places are more than 3,000 feet deep. Oceanographers have explored only a small fraction of the areas covered by oceans. "With the methods we use," oceanographer Frederic Grassle says, "we wouldn't even have discovered elephants if we were working on land." In fact, in the past few years some large marine animals have been found that researchers did not know existed. Not long ago 130-foot-long jellyfish were discovered off the coast of California. In 1938 fishermen in the waters off the coast of South Africa discovered a coelacanth, a fish almost seven feet long that scientists believed had been extinct for 70 million years.

In light of such finds it is not impossible that there really are huge sea serpents. The giant squids of Newfoundland are probably not even the largest of their kind. Some researchers speculate that there may be giant squids more than 130 feet long living in the depths of the oceans where light never reaches.

What is the Loch Ness Monster?

Loch Ness is a dark, cold lake in Scotland, 22 miles long and more than 650 feet deep. Many say a monster lives in it. Descriptions of the mysterious creature are amazingly similar to those of animals believed long extinct.

The creature was first mentioned in the year 565. Further sightings were reported in 1872 and 1903. The first newspaper report is from May 2, 1933. On a sunny afternoon a couple saw a 20-foot-long creature with two large, black humps swimming through the water about 1,000 feet away. News of the "Loch Ness Monster" went around the world and since then many people claim to have seen its "swan-like neck that it stretches up to seven feet out of the water and a dark gray body almost 30 feet long." In 1934 a man claimed to have photographed the monster. The picture was out of focus but was considered the best evidence so far.

Biologists have long doubted the existence of the Loch Ness Monster. If there really were such a creature, there would not be just one but many — males, females, and perhaps young ones. According to the biologists' calculations, however, the lake could not supply enough food for so many animals.

Is there really a Yeti in the Himalayan Mountains?

A strange being is said to live in the deserted, snow covered peaks of the Himalayan Mountains between India and Tibet. The Tibetans call the mysterious, frightening creature Kangui. The Nepalese call it Yeti. In English it is sometimes called the "abominable snowman." Descriptions claim that it is about 6 feet 8 inches tall, stands upright, and looks like an ape or a human covered with reddish-brown hair.

Zoologists first learned of its possible existence in 1832. The Englishman B. H. Hodgson reported that his native baggage carriers had fled from a large, ape-like creature they encountered high up in the mountains. A few times since 1832 American and European scientists have seen the creature from a distance, and even found hair and excrements, but they have never produced reliable photographs. For this reason many zoologists do not believe the Yeti actually exists. They suspect that the tracks might be from a Tibetan

THE MOST FAMOUS PHOTO of "Nessie" (see above) was taken in 1934. Just recently, the man who took it admitted that it was a fake. Shortly before he died, the photographer said that he had made a dummy and floated it in the lake and had then photographed it to play a joke on the newspapers. The "best evidence" has turned out to be a hoax.

Loch Ness in Scotland – many people think it is the home of a great sea monster.

THE YETI first came to the attention of zoologists in 1832. An Englishman climbing in the Himalayans, B. H. Hodgson, reported that his native baggage carriers had run away from a large ape-like creature high up in the mountains. He himself had not seen it, however. About 50 years later another explorer, Major L. A. Waddell, found giant footprints at an altitude of 5,000 feet. His guides assured him they were the tracks of the Yeti. Similar footprints were even photographed by English mountain climber Eric Shipton in 1951.

Russian professor G. Pronin drew this picture of the "abominable snowman." He claimed he had seen the creature in the Pamir Mountains in Afghanistan.

bear and look very large only because the heat of the Sun has melted away the edges. The Tibetan bear is about 6 feet 8 inches tall, has reddish-brown fur, and occasionally stands upright. Other biologists say that there once was a type of ape in Asia that grew to be over 8 feet tall. They believe it became extinct more than 500,000 years ago. It is possible, however, that some specimens have survived and are living in the high valleys of the Himalayan Mountains.

There is a special branch of science devoted to seeking out animals that we have not yet discovered. It is called cryptozoology (from the Greek kryptos = hidden). Cryptozoologists collect reports from eyewitnesses and construct as exact a picture of the animal as possible, and then set out to find it in nature.

> **Have we discovered all of the animals on Earth?**

There actually are animals that scientists believed were mythical until specimens were discovered and they were able to examine them. In Rwanda in East Africa, farmers told hunters stories of gigantic, screaming apes that swung from tree to tree. The hunters thought this was superstition until 1901, when a hunter killed one of these mountain gorillas.

The pygmy hippopotamus, the okapi, the dragon lizards of Komodo, and the giant panda were all once considered mythical animals. It was not until 1994 that researchers discovered the Vu-Quang ox and the giant muntjac — a large deer — in remote parts of Laos and

Vietnam. Until then scientists had only eyewitness accounts of the deer, a couple of horns, and a piece of a hide. Although these animals are not exactly small they managed to escape the notice of zoologists for many years.

For centuries people really believed there were unicorns — like the one shown here on a French tapestry (15th century).

There are no fire-breathing dragons, however, and no mermaids, no flying horses, no giant apes like King Kong, and no Godzilla. The Yeti, the unicorn, the Loch Ness Monster, and giant sea serpents all probably belong in the same category as UFOs, Atlantis, and ghosts.

Scientists remain skeptical because of the lack of evidence. "If you claimed to have a goat in your backyard, I might believe you," the popular science writer Martin Gardner once said, "but if you claim there's a unicorn in your backyard, I wouldn't believe it even if you showed me a picture. I would not rest until I had seen it with my own eyes."

Index

A

abominable snowman (see ⇨Yeti)
afterlife p. 38
aliens pp. 3, 9
Antarctica p. 23
Antikythera, computer of p. 17
astrology and astrologers pp. 24, 25, 26, 27, 28, 32, 36
astronomy pp. 6, 26
Atlantis pp. 13, 14, 15, 16
    description pp. 13, 14
    location p. 13
atomic energy, atomic bombs pp. 11, 15
augury and augurs p. 29

B

Bermuda Triangle p. 13
Bible p. 11
Boleyn, Ann p. 33

C

card-reading p. 30
centaurs p. 47
coelacanths p. 46
Columbus, Christopher pp. 22, 23
Cook, Captain James p. 23
Coyne, Larry p. 7
cryptozoology p. 47

D

Daniken, Erich von pp. 10, 11, 12
Delphi, Greece (see ⇨Oracle at Delphi)
demons p. 5
dowsing and dowsers pp. 42, 43
divining rods pp. 42, 43
druids p. 16

E

earthquakes p. 29
Easter Islands pp. 11, 12
ectoplasm p. 39
exploration, ancient p. 20
Extrasensory perception pp. 15, 40
extraterrestrial beings pp. 8, 9, 10, 11, 12

F

Finaeus, Oronteus p. 23
Flying Dutchman, The p. 37
flying horses p. 47
fortune-telling and fortune-tellers pp. 28, 29, 30, 32

G

gene technology p. 10
ghosts pp. 33, 35, 37, 47
ghost hunters p. 39
ghost ships p. 37
gods pp. 5, 10
Godzilla p. 47
Gorilla p. 47

H

hallucinations p. 39
hauntings p. 39
hereafter (see ⇨afterlife)
Heyerdahl, Thor pp. 12, 21
Homer p. 13
horoscopes pp. 26, 27, 28

I

I Ching p. 30

K

King Kong p. 47
Kraken (see ⇨squid, giant)
kuei (see ⇨spirits, Chinese)

L

Loch Ness monster pp. 46, 47

M

magicians p. 39
maps pp. 22, 23
Maya pp. 15, 17
medicine men p. 38
mediums pp. 36, 37, 39
mermaids p. 47
monsters pp. 35, 45, 46, 47
Moon p. 27
Moses p. 11

N

Noah p. 10
Nostradamus p. 32

O

Oracle at Delphi pp. 30, 31
Ouija p. 38

P

palm reading and palm readers p. 30
pandas, giant p. 47
parapsychology pp. 40, 41
Phoenicians pp. 19, 20
Plato pp. 13, 14, 15
poltergeists p. 35
psi pp. 40, 41
Ptolemy, Claudius p. 26
pyramids pp. 10, 17
Pytheas p. 20

Pythia (see also ⇨Oracle at Delphi) pp. 30, 31

R

Reis, Piri pp. 22, 23
Rhine, Joseph B. p. 41
Roswell, New Mexico p. 6

S

sailors and seafarers pp. 13, 19, 20, 21
science fiction
    movies p. 9
    depiction of aliens pp. 3, 8, 9
sea serpents p. 46
séances pp. 35, 38, 39, 40
Shakespeare, William p. 24
shamans p. 39
shen (see ⇨spirits, Chinese)
space travelers pp. 10, 12, 15, 47
spaceships and spacecrafts pp. 4, 5, 9, 11, 12
spirits (see also ⇨ghosts) pp. 33, 36, 37, 38, 39, 40
    Chinese p. 35
    Japanese p. 36
spiritualism pp. 37, 38
squid, giant pp. 46, 47
Star Trek p. 9
Star Wars p. 9
stargazers (see ⇨astrology and astrologers)
Stonehenge
    trilithons p. 16
    Sarsen circle p. 16

T

Tarot cards p. 30
technology, ancient
    astronomical computer p. 17
    electric battery p. 18
Tower of London p. 33

U

UFO pp. 4, 5, 6, 7, 47
    abductions of p. 5
    explanations of pp. 6, 7
    sightings p. 5
unicorns p. 47

W

witches p. 16

Y

Yeti pp. 46, 47

Z

Zodiac pp. 25, 26, 27, 28